18 Vetulicolians

EVERYONE SHOULD KNOW ABOUT

STANTON F. FINK

VOLUME VIII OF STANTON'S COLORING BOOKS

Acknowledgments

and Dedication

To my father, in whose books I discovered my first monsters.

To Will Caligan, whose help and encouragement is one of the primary reasons for this coloring book's existence.

To Mariano Silvera, who should have had his own artbooks

To Doctor David Morafka, who helped teach me to be more picky with my information.

To my friends, who helped push me to make this.

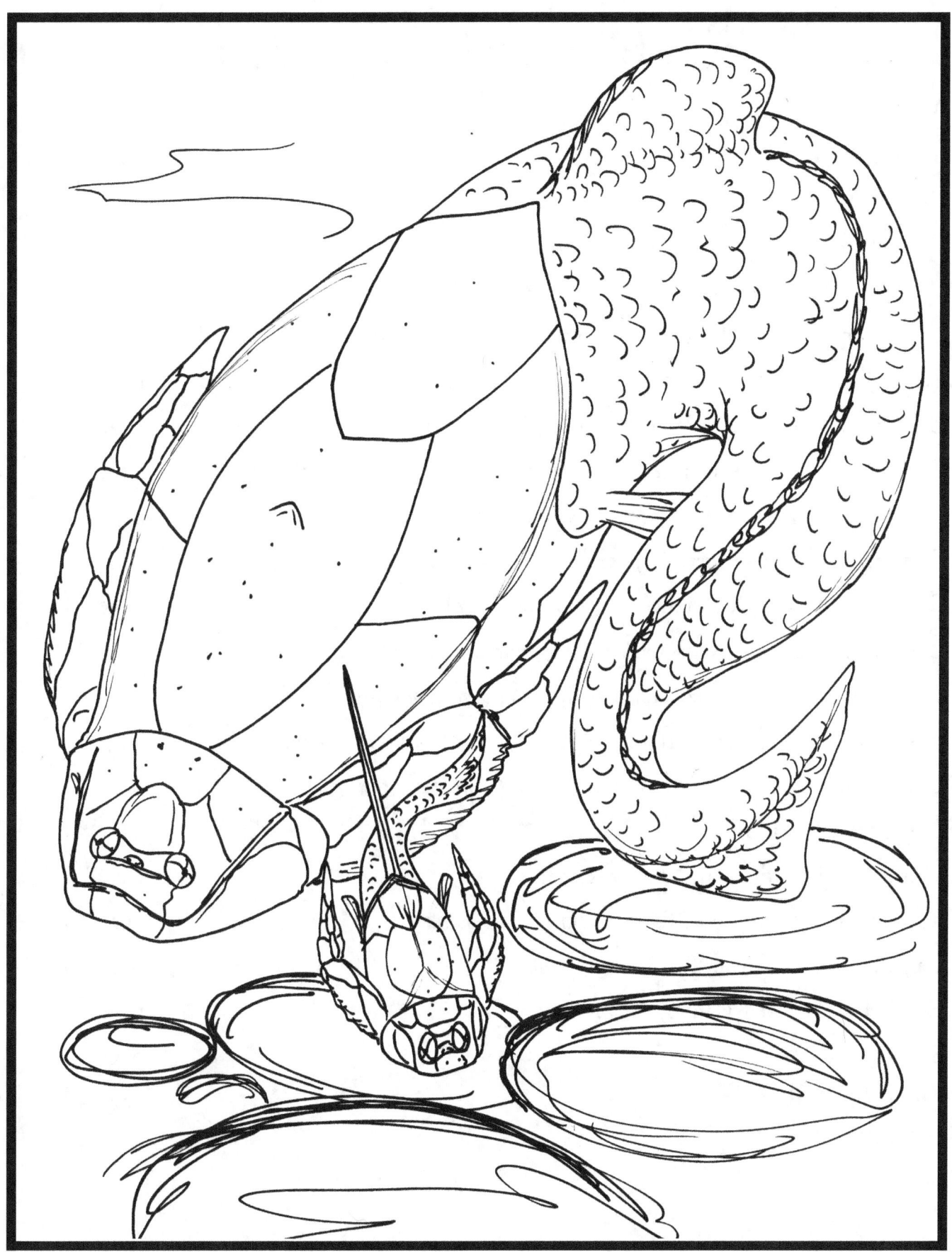

Table of Contents

Introduction

The Vetulicolians are an obscure group of extinct deuterostomes who are, as far as we humans know, temporally restricted to the Cambrian Period of the Palaeozoic Era. How these mysterious animals relate to modern animals has long vexed researchers ever since it was determined that *Vetulicola cuneata*, the wedgefaced ancientworm, was actually not a bivalved arthropod. Thorough anatomical comparisons and various fossils revealing the presence of notochords, researchers eventually determined that vetulicolians were chordates related to the tunicates and larvaceans of Urochordata.

While most of the other coloring books in this series contain 17 entries, I've made an exception with this volume, as vetulicolians are near and dear to my heart and my career as an amateur prehistoric animal artist.

Glossary

- **Aquatic**- Living in water.
- **Arthropod**- Any member of the animal phylum Arthropoda, including trilobites, arachnids, crustaceans, insects, myriapods and their relatives. All arthropods have armor-like, jointed exoskeletons made of chitin-derived plates, sometimes reinforced with calcium carbonate, and jointed limbs.
- **Cambrian**- A period of time in the Paleozoic Era from 541 to 485 million years ago.
- **Carapace**- A shell or shell-like structure that encloses either the thorax or entire forebody of an animal. Depending on the size, the carapace may also enclose the entire body, as well.
- **Chordate**- Any member of the animal phylum Chordata, including sea squirts, lancet fish, and vertebrates (such as lampreys, sharks, tuna, frogs, lizards, chickens, and people). All chordates have, at least at some point in their life cycle, a notochord, a long, flexible rod, usually made of cartilage, or, in the case of most vertebrates, cartilage and bone, running down the back from head to tail, directly beneath the neural tube.
- **Cnidarian**- Any member of the animal phylum Cnidaria, such as jellyfish, box jellies, Portuguese Man'o'war, sea anemones, coral and the parasitic myxozoans. Cnidarians are usually radially symmetrical, and have unique, venom-injecting stinging cells called "cnidocytes."
- **Ediacaran**- The last period of time in the Precambrian Eon from 635 to 542 million years ago.
- **Fauna**- In an ecological context, "fauna" refers to the animal components of an ecosystem.
- **Formation**- In a geological or paleontological context, a formation is a group of rock layers.
- ***Incertae sedis***- A Latin phrase literally meaning "uncertain seat." *"Incertae sedis"* is a term in classification used to refer to a species or group whose relationships with related organisms are unclear or poorly defined.
- **Mesozoic**- An era of time in the Phanerozoic Eon from 249 to 66 million years ago.
- **Nekton**- Any aquatic animal that lives either entirely or almost entirely in the water column, and relies on its own swimming or propulsion abilities to keep and move itself in and around the water column. Anchovies, porpoises and ichthyosaurs are examples of nekton.
- **Paleozoic**- An era of time in the Phanerozoic Eon from 249 to 66 million years ago.
- **Pharynx**- A structure in the throat of many animals located directly behind the mouth or oral chamber. In vertebrates, it often houses breathing structures, like gills.
- **Plankton**- An organism that uses water currents and waterflow to as its primary means of transportation in the water column because it is either too small to move long distances by its own power, or lacks the ability to propel itself entirely. Sargassum

seaweed and jellyfish are two varieties of plankton.
- **Terrestrial**- Living on land.
- **Urochordate**- A subgroup of chordates that include the tunicates and the larvaceans. Tunicates have a larval stage that looks a lot like an eyeless tadpole: larvaceans do not metamorphosize out of this form, and that is why they are called "larvaceans."

Name	# Geriatric Egg
Species	*Ooedigera peeli*
Phylum	Chordata
Subphylum	Vetulicolia
Class	Vetulicolida
Family	Vetulicolidae
Size	Holotype specimen 4 centimeters long
Time Period	"Stage 3" of the Early Cambrian, between 519 to 516 million years ago.
Location	Buen Formation, Sirius Passet, Greenland
Comments	The Geriatric Egg, *Ooedigera peeli,* is a tadpole-like vetulicolid from the Sirius Passet Lagerstätte, its fossils dating from about 523 million years ago. So far, it is known only from a 4 centimeter long specimen. Because the leaf-shaped tail moves side to side, the geriatric egg superficially resembles the geosciencefishes of Didazoonidae. That the carapace divides into a dorsal half and a ventral half places *O. peeli* squarely within Vetulicolidae. Small, wart-like tubercules are spread in a random distribution across the surface of the carapace and cuticle. The way in which the fossil appears to be squished suggests that the cuticle of the living animal was much softer than the cuticle of either *Vetulicola* or *Beidazoon*.

The geriatric egg lived sympatrically with another variety of vetulicolid in Sirius Passet, but, this second variety has not yet been officially described or named.

The picture depicts a geriatric egg being menaced by the nightmare anomalocaridid, *Pambdelurion*.

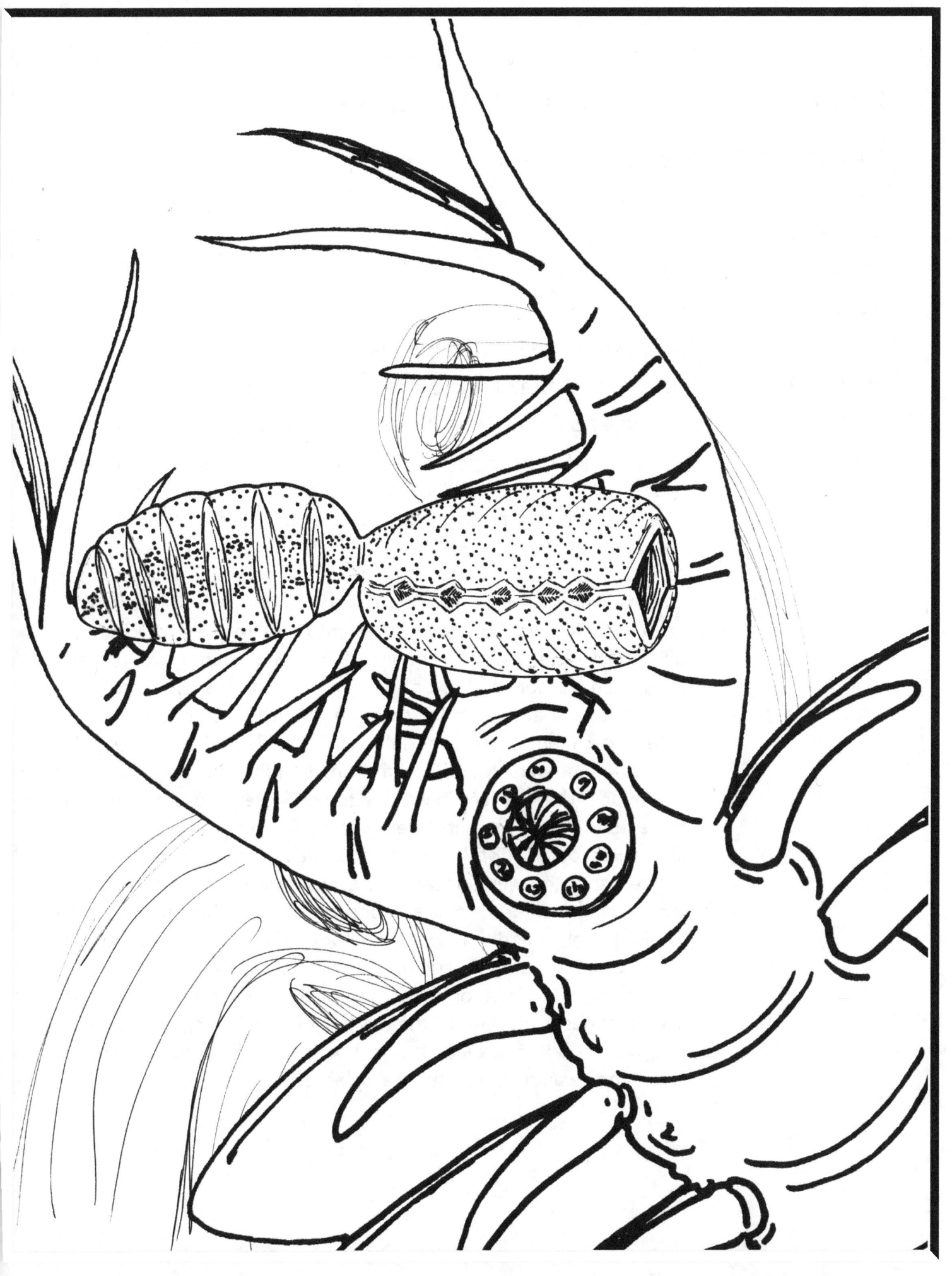

Name	Wedgefaced Ancientworm
Species	*Vetulicola cuneata*
Phylum	Chordata
Subphylum	Vetulicolia
Class	Vetulicolida
Family	Vetulicolidae
Size	Average length of 9 centimeters
Time Period	"Stage 3" of the Cambrian Period, 515 million years ago
Location	Chengjiang County, Yunnan Province, China
Comments	

The Wedgefaced Ancientworm, *Vetulicola cuneata*, is the type species of the genus and of Vetulicolia as a whole. This animal, which was similar in size to a large feeder goldfish, was originally described as a "bivalved crustacean," but, the articulation of the carapace was unlike anything seen in any arthropods. The posterior corner comes to a spine-like point, and the dorsal crest is large and recurved. The oral disk is stretched into a beak-like structure. The gill opens were diamond-shaped. The living animal would have resembled a wooden clog or a pointed shoe converted into an ice skate, with an oar-shaped tail emerging from the top of the heel.

A few specimens of the wedgefaced (and, later, of the rectangular ancientworm) were found to have small epibionts growing at the posterior end of the terminal tail segment, in very close proximity to the anus. These epibionts, identified as the putative, echinoderm-like entoproctan *Cotyledion tylodes*, lead some researchers to suggest that the wedgefaced was a burrowing organism, and that the epibionts settled on the exposed tail-tip. The nature of the fossils' burial, in addition to the anatomy of vetulicolians in general both strongly suggest against a burrowing lifestyle. A more parsimonious explanation is that the planktonic larvae of *C. tylodes* serendipitously attached to the tail-tips of vetulicolids, and survived into adulthood on a diet of their host's feces in a very thorough, "waste not, want not" commensal symbiosis.

Name	Rectangular Ancientworm
Species	*Vetulicola rectangulata*
Phylum	Chordata
Subphylum	Vetulicolia
Class	Vetulicolida
Family	Vetulicolidae
Size	Average length of 7.5 centimeters
Time Period	"Stage 3" of the Cambrian Period, 515 million years ago (Maybe from 516 million years ago)
Location	Chengjiang County, Yunnan Province, China, and possibly the Mural Formation of Jasper National Park, Alberta, Canada
Comments	The Rectangular Ancientworm, *Vetulicola rectangulata,* is a species of vetulicolid closely related to the wedgefaced and pearl string ancientworms . Fossils of *V. rectangulata* are found only in the Haikou locality, in Yunnan, and possibly from the Mural Formation of Jasper National Park in Canada (which would make it the only ancientworm found outside of China). It differs from both species by being smaller (average total length of adult specimens is about 7.5 centimeters). The rectangular differs from the pearl string by having a smooth carapace, and differs from the wedgefaced in that the oral disk does not project out into a prominent beak, and that the posterior portion of the ventral keel lacks a spine-like projection. The living animal would have had a rounded cylindrical forebody that, when squished flat as a fossil, gives it a rectangular outline. The rectangular's gill openings are large diamond-shapes. Some researchers have been skeptical over whether the rectangular and the wedgefaced are distinct species, noting that the differences in proportions and anatomies may possibly be due to different growth stages and or post-mortem damage. Such arguments have been unconvincing, though, as hundreds of specimens have been found, permitting exquisitely detailed analyses of both species' anatomical differences, differences that currently do not suggest different genders.

Name   Pearl String Ancientworm

Species	*Vetulicola monile*
Phylum	Chordata
Subphylum	Vetulicolia
Class	Vetulicolida
Family	Vetulicolidae
Size	Holotype about 6 centimeters, whole animal may be up to 9 centimeters long.
Time Period	"Stage 3" of the Cambrian Period, 515 million years ago
Location	Heilinpu Formation of the Yu'anshan Member near Mafang, of Haikou, in Chengjiang County, Yunnan Province, China
Comments	The Pearl String Ancientworm, *Vetulicola monile,* is known from an incomplete specimen from the Heilinpu Formation of the Yu'anshan Member near Mafang, Haikou, in Yunnan. The fossil specimen shows a 6 centimeter long carapace very similar to those seen in the rectangular ancientworm, except that the carapace of *V. monile* has several rows of raised tubercles running longitudinally. The specific name translates as "string of pearls," alluding to how the living animal, which was bulkier than *V. cuneata*, would have looked like it was wrapped in strings of pearls.

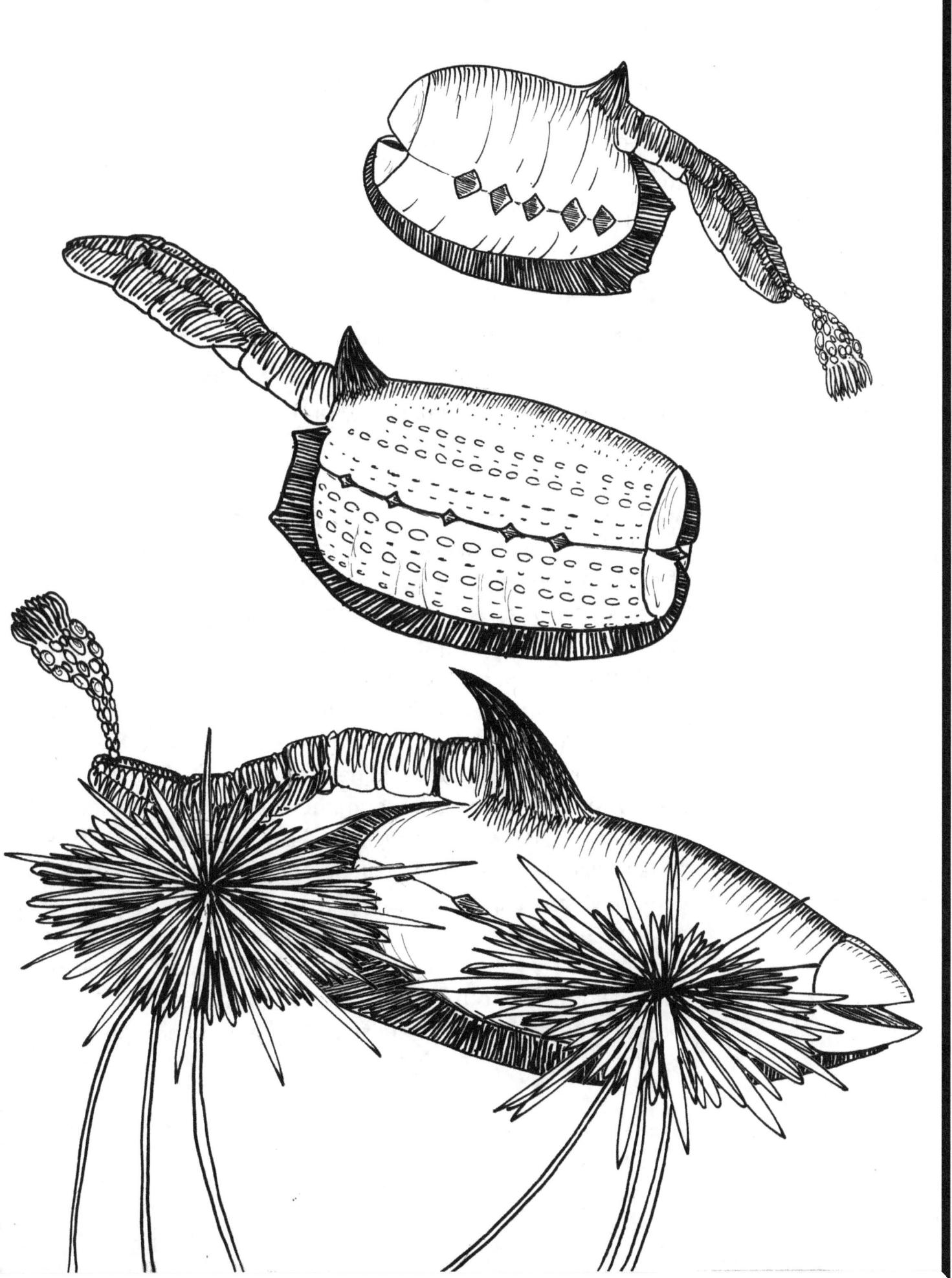

Name	Gantoucun Ancientworm
Species	*Vetulicola gantoucunensis*
Phylum	Chordata
Subphylum	Vetulicolia
Class	Vetulicolida
Family	Vetulicolidae
Size	Average length of 9.5 centimeters
Time Period	"Stage 3" of the Cambrian Period, 515 million years ago
Location	Gantoucun, near Kunming, Chengjiang County, Yunnan Province, China
Comments	At an averagle length of 9.5 centimeters, the Gantoucun Ancientworm, *Vetulicola gantoucunensis,* is the largest member of the genus, and is the third largest vetulicolian after the Magnifiworm and the Island Swimmer. Fossils of *V. gantoucunensis* are found from the Guanshan Fauna locality in Kunming. The first specimens were found near the village of Gantoucun, a suburb of Kunming.

The Gantoucun ancientworm differs from the rectangular ancientworm by the former's larger size and more massive proportions, as well as a prominent point on the dorsal fin of the posterior-most tail segment joining the anterior forebody. *V. gantoucunensis* also differs from the rectangular in that the tail joins the forebody more anteriorly, so that, in the living animal, the tail appears to emanate from the middle of the creature's back. In this respect, it is very similar to the Dragon's Treasure ancientworm, the other vetulicolid of the Guanshan Fauna locality. The gill openings are shaped like oval knotholes.

Name	Dragon's Treasure Ancientworm
Species	*Vetulicola longbaoshanensis*
Phylum	Chordata
Subphylum	Vetulicolia
Class	Vetulicolida
Family	Vetulicolidae
Size	Average lenth of 8 centimeters
Time Period	"Stage 3" of the Cambrian Period, 515 million years ago
Location	Canglangpu Formation near Yilu Village in Chengjiang County, Yunnan Province, China
Comments	

The Dragon's Treasure Ancientworm, *Vetulicolia longbaoshanensis,* is the second vetulicolid from the Kunming locality of the Guanshan Faunal Stage of the Maotianshan Shales after the Gantoucun Ancientworm. The first specimens were found near "Dragon's Treasure Hill," Longbao Shan (龍寶山). The average length is 8 centimeters. The forebody is barrel-shaped: *V. longbaoshanensis* differs dramatically from *V. rectangulata* by the differently shaped ventral keel which shortens in height near the anterior portion, and by the five pairs of star-shaped gill openings. The attachment site of the tail to the forebody is position much more anteriorly than any other member in the genus, save for *V. gantoucunensis.* These similarities, together with both species being found in the same locality, have lead a few researchers to postulate that *V. longbaoshanensis* may represent a subadult stage of *V. gantoucunensis.*

The dragon's treasure ancientworm is known from numerous specimens the Wulongqing Member of the Lower Cambrian Canglangpu Formation near Yilu Village in Yunnan.

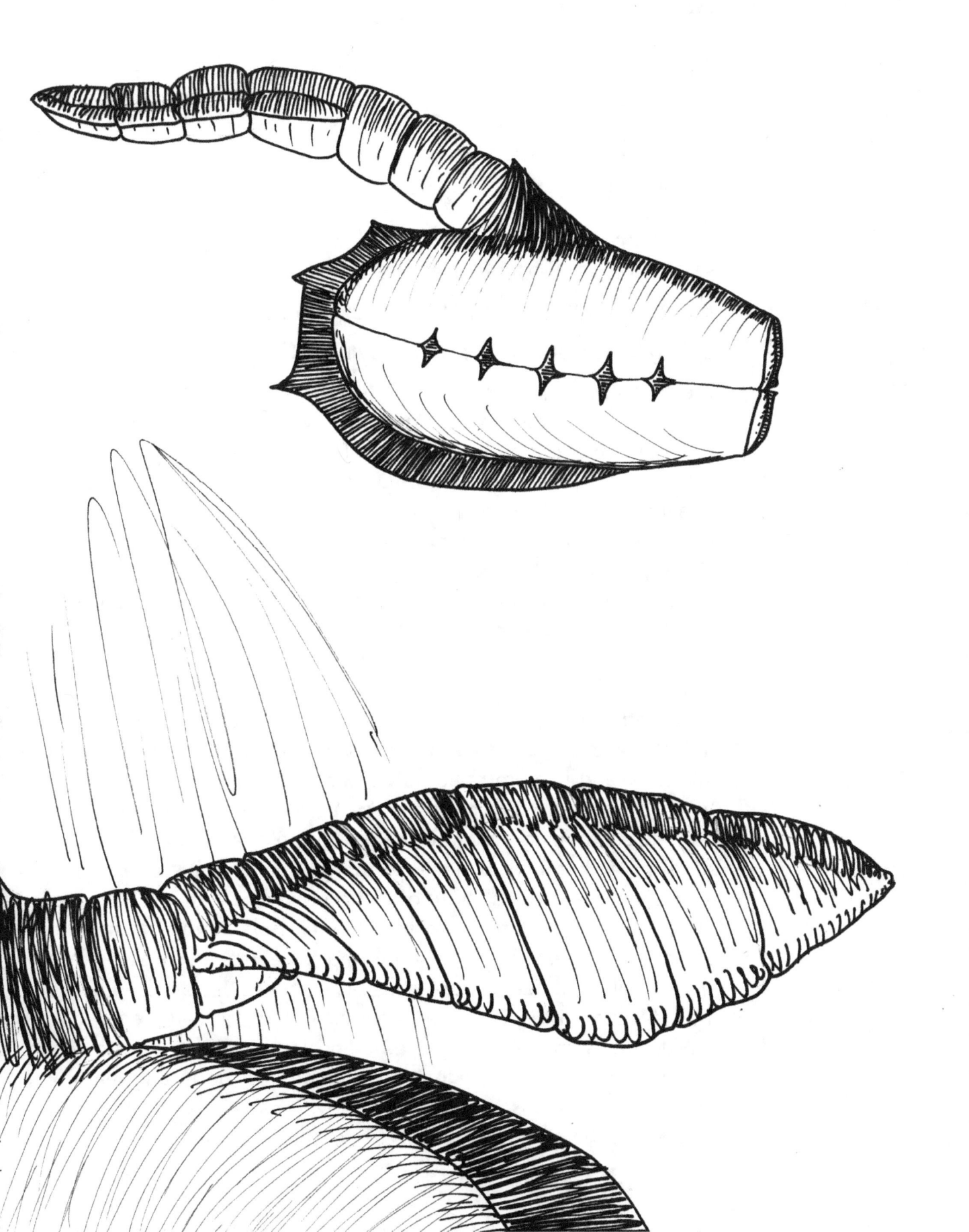

Name	Beautiworm
Species	*Beidazoon venustum*
Phylum	Chordata
Subphylum	Vetulicolia
Class	Vetulicolida
Family	Vetulicolidae
Size	Ranging from 8 to 14 millimeters
Time Period	"Stage 3" of the Cambrian Period, 515 million years ago
Location	Chengjiang County, Yunnan Province, China
Comments	The Beautiworm, *Beidazoon venustum* is the smallest known vetulicolian, with the smallest known individuals being 8 millimeters in length: the largest individuals of *B. venustum* are up to 14 millimeters. Fossils are known from the Haikou and Guanshan localities of the Maotianshan Shales.

The generic name is a compound of the Chinese abbreviation of "Peking University," "北大" and "zoon," or animal. The specific name is derived from a Latin word meaning "Of Venus," in reference to how wondrously beautiful Shu Degan found their fossils.

The appearance of the beautiworm is very similar to that of the rectangular or pearl string ancientworms, albeit, one three-hundredth the size of the rectangular, or one one-hundredth the size of *Didazoon*. The forebody is covered in crowded rows of small tubercles, and is more noticeably segmented than the forebody of *Vetulicola* species. Similar to *Vetulicola*, the beautiworm has a long ventral keel running down the median line of the forebody's ventral surface. A flattened, paddle-like tail of seven segments attaches near the posterior-most point of the forebody.

Aldridge, et. al, described them as "*Bullivetula variola*," remarking that the creatures' small size suggested they were juveniles, as they were similar in size to other fossils thought to be of juvenile individuals of *Vetulicola*. That there have been no vetulicolian of a similar appearance to *B. venustum*, and larger than 14 millimeters yet found made Aldridge stop short of officially suggesting that the fossils of *B. venustum* represent juveniles, instead, ultimately agreeing with Shu that the fossils represent tiny adults.

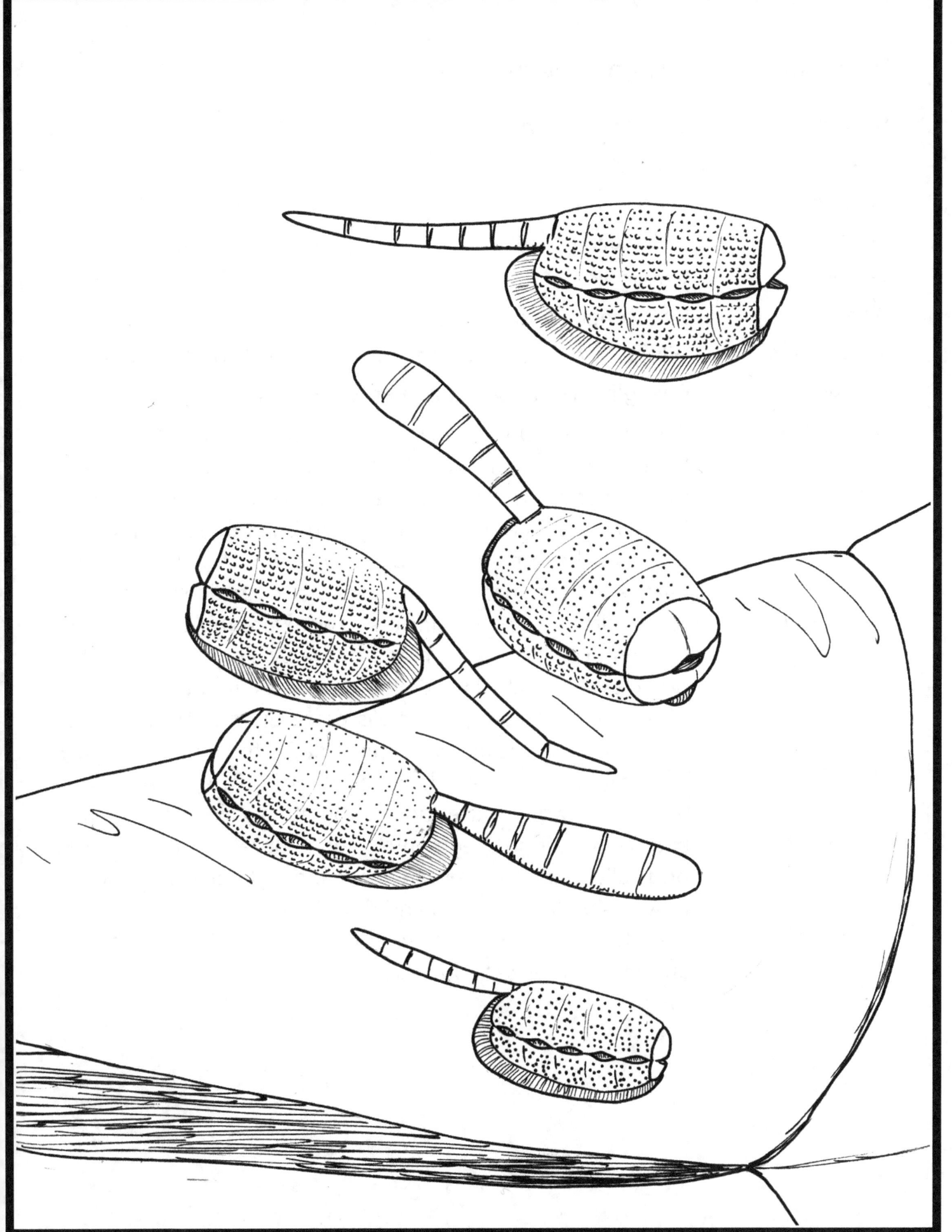

Name	Magnifiworm
Species	*Yuyuanozoon magnificissimi*
Phylum	Chordata
Subphylum	Vetulicolia
Class	Vetulicolida
Family	Vetulicolidae
Size	20.2 centimeters
Time Period	"Stage 3" of the Cambrian Period, 515 million years ago
Location	Chengjiang County, Yunnan Province, China
Comments	The Magnifiworm, *Yuyuanozoon magnificissimi,* is the largest known chordate from the Cambrian, the only known fossil specimen measuring a whopping 20.2 centimeters long. Its fossil is from the Early Cambrian of Yunnan, China, as a member of the Chengjiang Fauna. The closest living relatives of the magnifiworm and other vetulicolians are the sea squirts. The magnifiworm swam around in the water column near the seafloor, and probably siphoned up edible particles as it sucked water into its pinhole mouth.

Although the fossil specimen is perfectly preserved (sort of, what with it being squashed flat), the magnifiworm's anatomy provides few clues about its lifestyle. When alive, the animal would have looked something like a segmented egg with a long, segmented tail. Because the tail was originally cylindrical, researchers cannot determine if the tail moved side to side or up and down.

Here two magnifiworms are compared with the rectangular ancientworm, *V. rectangulata.*

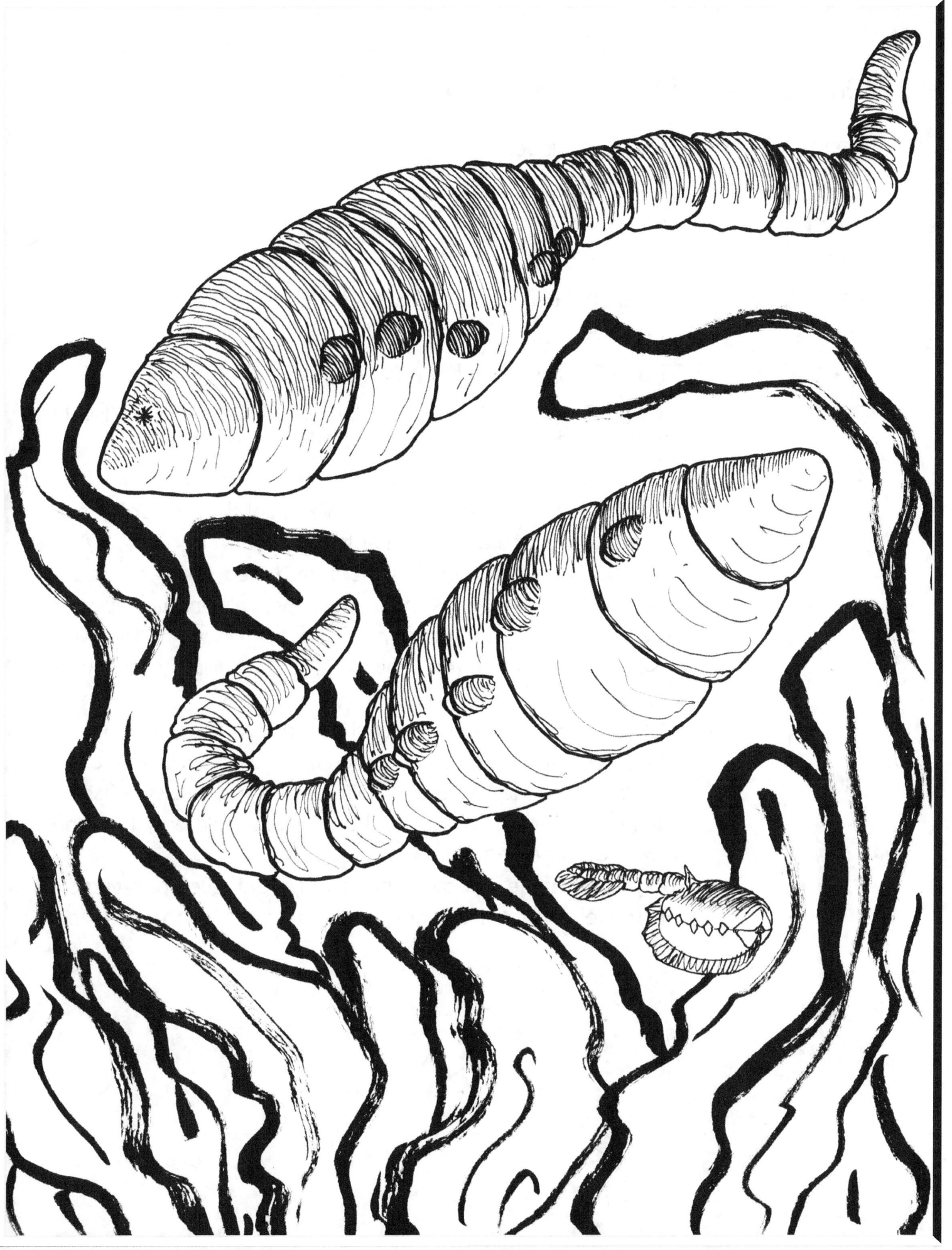

Name	Hao's Geosciencefish
Species	*Didazoon haoae*
Phylum	Chordata
Subphylum	Vetulicolia
Class	Vetulicolida
Family	Didazoonidae
Size	6 to 10 centimeters long
Time Period	"Stage 3" of the Cambrian Period, 515 million years ago
Location	Qiongzhusi Formation, Yu'anshan Member (Eoredlichia zone), Chengjiang County, Yunnan Province, China
Comments	The geosciencefishes were closely related to the ancientworms of *Vetulicola* and Vetulicolidae, though, they differed by the cuticle of the anterior portion of the body be thin and flexible, rather than be a hardened carapace, and a large tail that moves from side to side, rather than up and down. The anterior portion of the body was hollow and voluminous, like all vetulicolids, probably housing the vast pharynx.

Miss (Y.) Hao's Geosciencefish, *Didazoon haoae*, has a crown-like oral disc, also characteristic of Didazoonidae. It differs from the covered and lamprey geosciencefishes, *Pomatrum* and *Xidazoon*, in that the oral disc only has one row of ornamentation.

The genus name is a combination of a Chinese abbreviation of "University of Geosciences (Beijing)," plus "zoon," meaning "animal." |

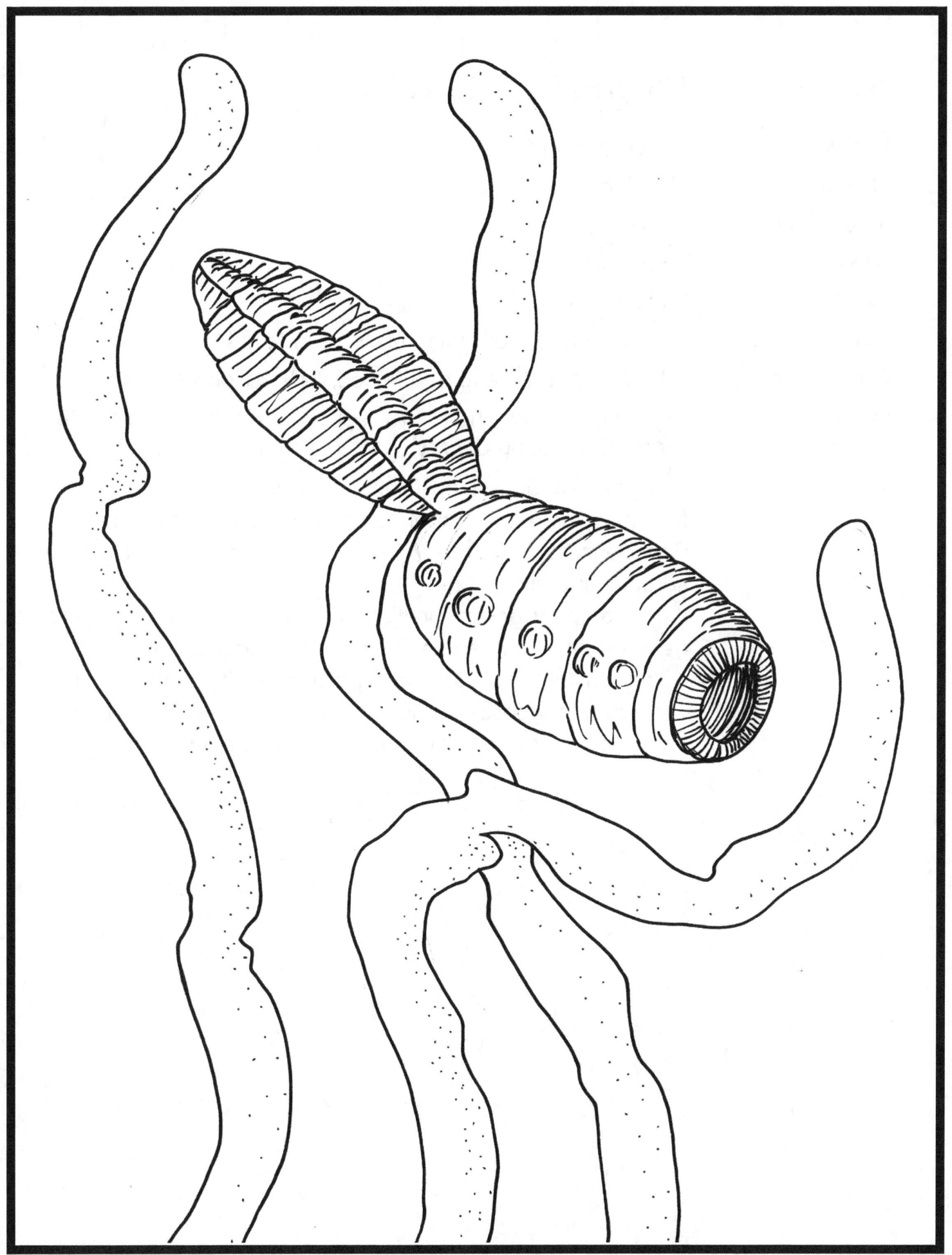

Name

Covered Geosciencefish

Species	*Pomatrum ventralis*
Phylum	Chordata
Subphylum	Vetulicolia
Class	Vetulicolida
Family	Didazoonidae
Size	Probably up to 9 or 10 centimeters in length
Time Period	"Stage 3" of the Cambrian Period, 515 million years ago
Location	Qiongzhusi Formation, Yu'anshan Member (Eoredlichia zone), Chengjiang County, Yunnan Province, China
Comments	The Covered Geosciencefish, *Pomatrum ventralis*, is known from a damaged, incomplete holotype, and, if the Lamprey Geosciencefish, *Xidazoon*, is not distinct from it, three additional fossils.

If the lamprey geosciencefish is distinct, then the covered geosciencefish had an oar-shaped tail, and possibly a hint of a keel on the posterior-most portion of the anterior body. The covered geosciencefish differs from Hao's in that the oral disc has two rows of tubercules ornamentating it.

Name	Lamprey Geosciencefish
Species	*Xidazoon stephanus*
Phylum	Chordata
Subphylum	Vetulicolia
Class	Vetulicolida
Family	Didazoonidae
Size	Probably up to 9 centimeters in length
Time Period	"Stage 3" of the Cambrian Period, 515 million years ago
Location	Qiongzhusi Formation, Yu'anshan Member (Eoredlichia zone), Chengjiang County, Yunnan Province, China
Comments	

The Lamprey or Crowned Geosciencefish, *Xidazoon stephanus*, is a didazoonid with a complexly ornamented oral disc and a large, leaf-shaped tail. When it was originally described, it was a mysterious *incertae sedis* that was compared to the Π fish, or "Pushmepullyou," *Pipiscus zangerli*, a peculiar lamprey from the Mazon Creek of Carboniferous Illinois. Now that the three known specimens have been better studied, the lamprey geosciencefish is now regarded as closely related to the covered geosciencefish, *Pomatrum*, to the point where several authorities regard *Xidazoon* as a junior synonym of *Pomatrum*. This synonymizing is justified on the fact that the ornamentation of the oral disc, a double row of tubercules, identical in both animals. Differences in anatomy, i.e., shape of the tails and body form, are waived away on the assumption that these differences were created by deformation during burial and fossilization.

The genus name refers to the Northwest University at Xi'an, in China.

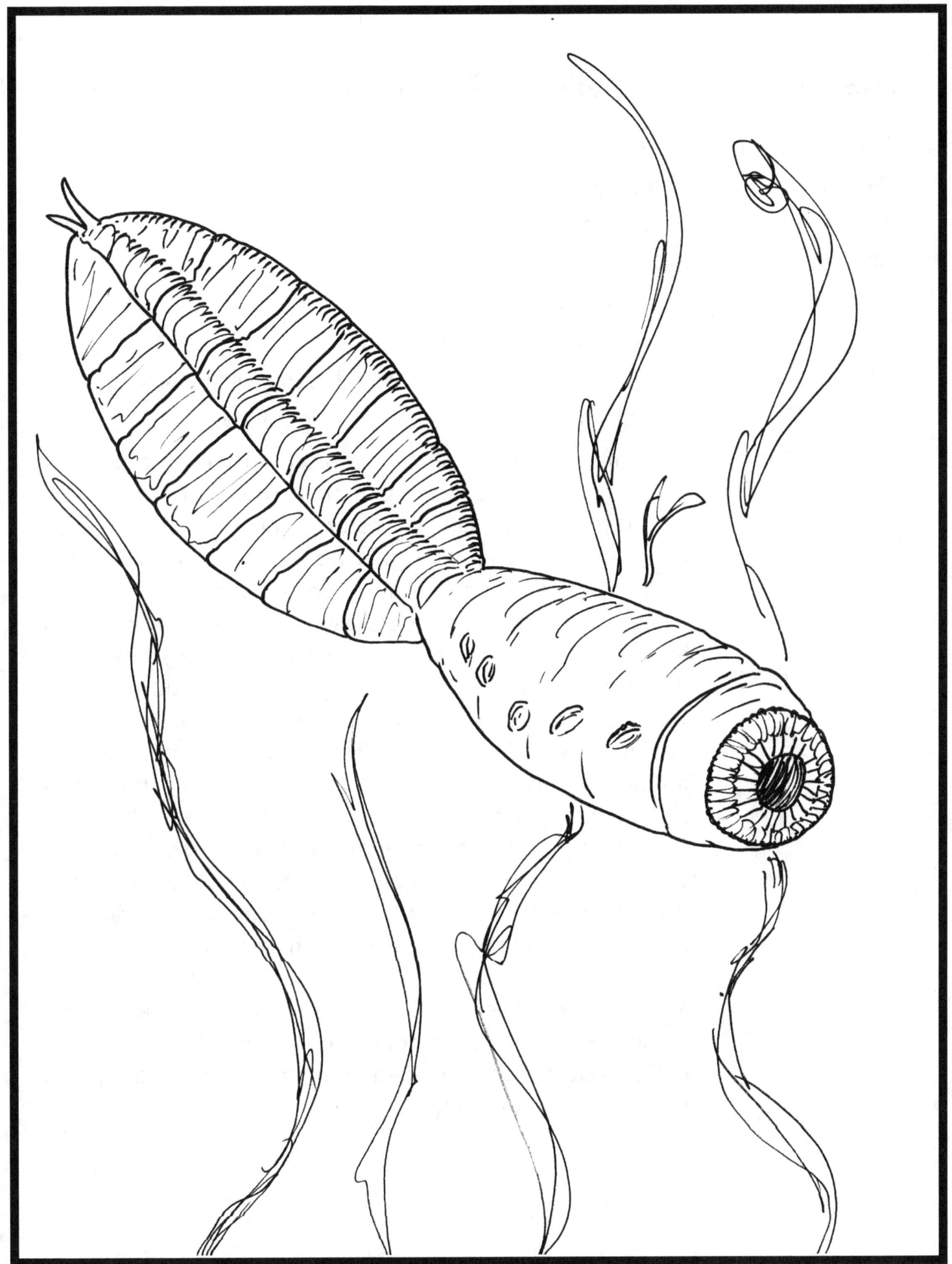

Name	Longtailed Differentworm
Species	*Hetermorphus longicaudatus*
Phylum	Chordata
Subphylum	Vetulicolia
Class	Heteromorphida
Family	Heteromorphidae
Size	About 5.5 centimeters long
Time Period	"Stage 3" of the Cambrian Period, 515 million years ago
Location	Chengjiang County, Yunnan Province, China
Comments	

The Differentworms of *Hetermorphus* have long been a headache to researchers of Cambrian deuterostomes. While it remains obvious that species of *Hetermorphus* are related to *Vetulicola* and other vetulicolians, where *Hetermorphus* sits in the tree of Vetulicolia has been a painfully protracted game of musical chairs, especially since the differentworms have been repeatedly placed in *Banffia* so many times that that genus should have a revolving door installed.

The main distinction between the differentworms and the banffiworms of Banffozoa is that differentworms have no distinct oral disc or crown, and that while both banffiworms and differentworms have many, many segments in their tails, the segmentation in the different worms have segmentation so fine so as to resemble wrinkling. Another important distinction is that banffiworms have cylindrical carapaces, while the differentworms have egg-shaped carapaces.

The Longtailed Differentworm, *Hetermorphus longicaudatus,* has a long, ribbon-shaped tail, and keels running along the dorsal ridge and the ventral ridge.

In this picture, two longtailed differentworms are compared to an individual of "Form A."

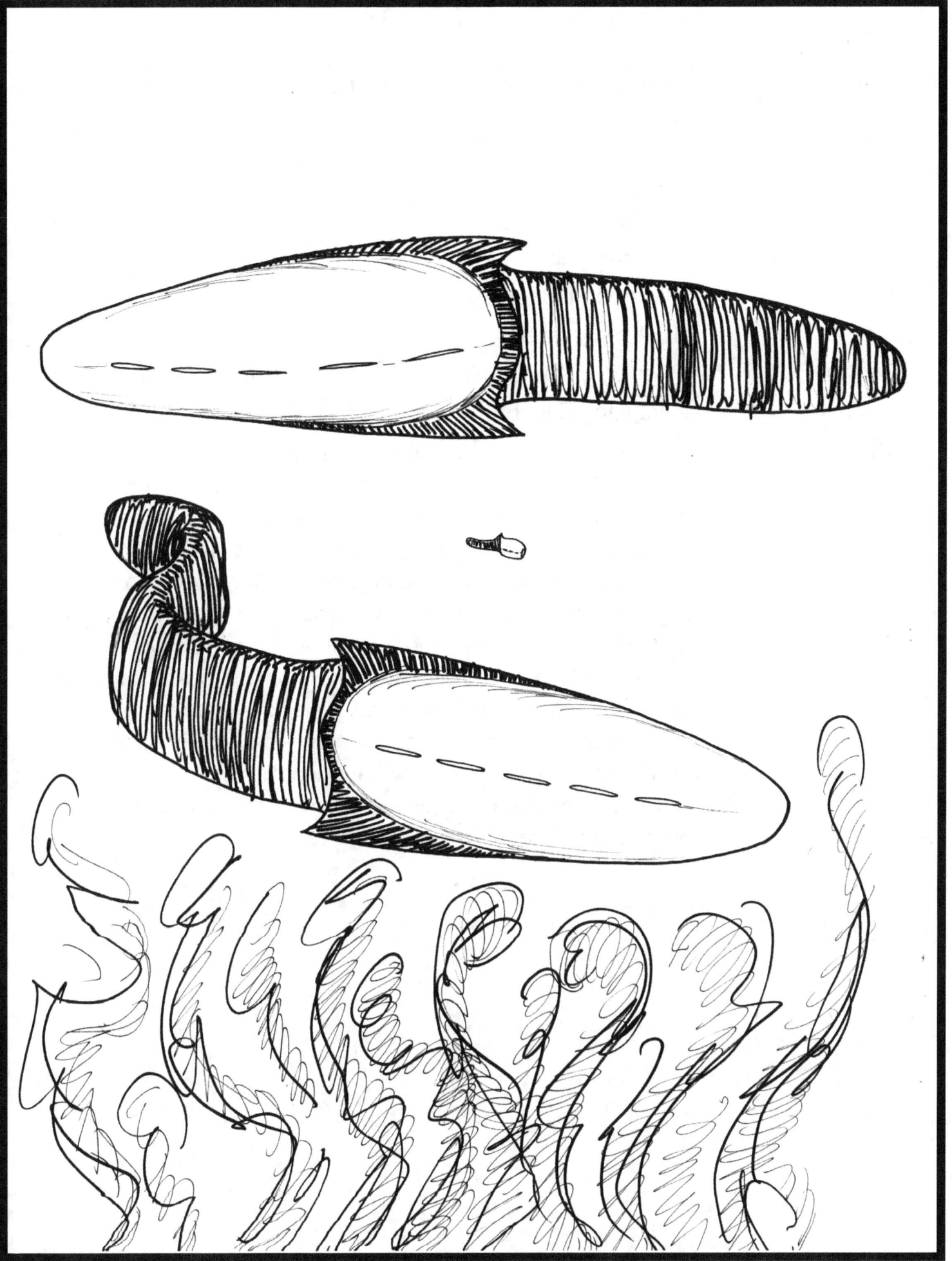

Name

Confusing Differentworm

Species	*Hetermorphus confusus*
Phylum	Chordata
Subphylum	Vetulicolia
Class	Heteromorphida
Family	Heteromorphidae
Size	3 to 4 centimeters
Time Period	"Stage 3" of the Cambrian Period, 515 million years ago
Location	Chengjiang County, Yunnan Province, China
Comments	The genus name *Hetermorphus* literally translates as "different form," in reference to the great variation seen in the specimens. This variation is also the reason why the Confusing Differentworm, *H. confusus*, was named as such. It differs from the Longtailed Differentworm, *H. longicaudatus*, primarily by its shorter, kite-shaped tail, and by how the keels on the dorsal and ventral ridges are reduced to sort of prominent corners on the posterior-most ends of the anterior carapace. This kite-shaped tail also causes many researchers to constantly assume it is nothing more than another species of banffiworm.

Here, two confusing differentworms are compared to a longtailed differentworm.

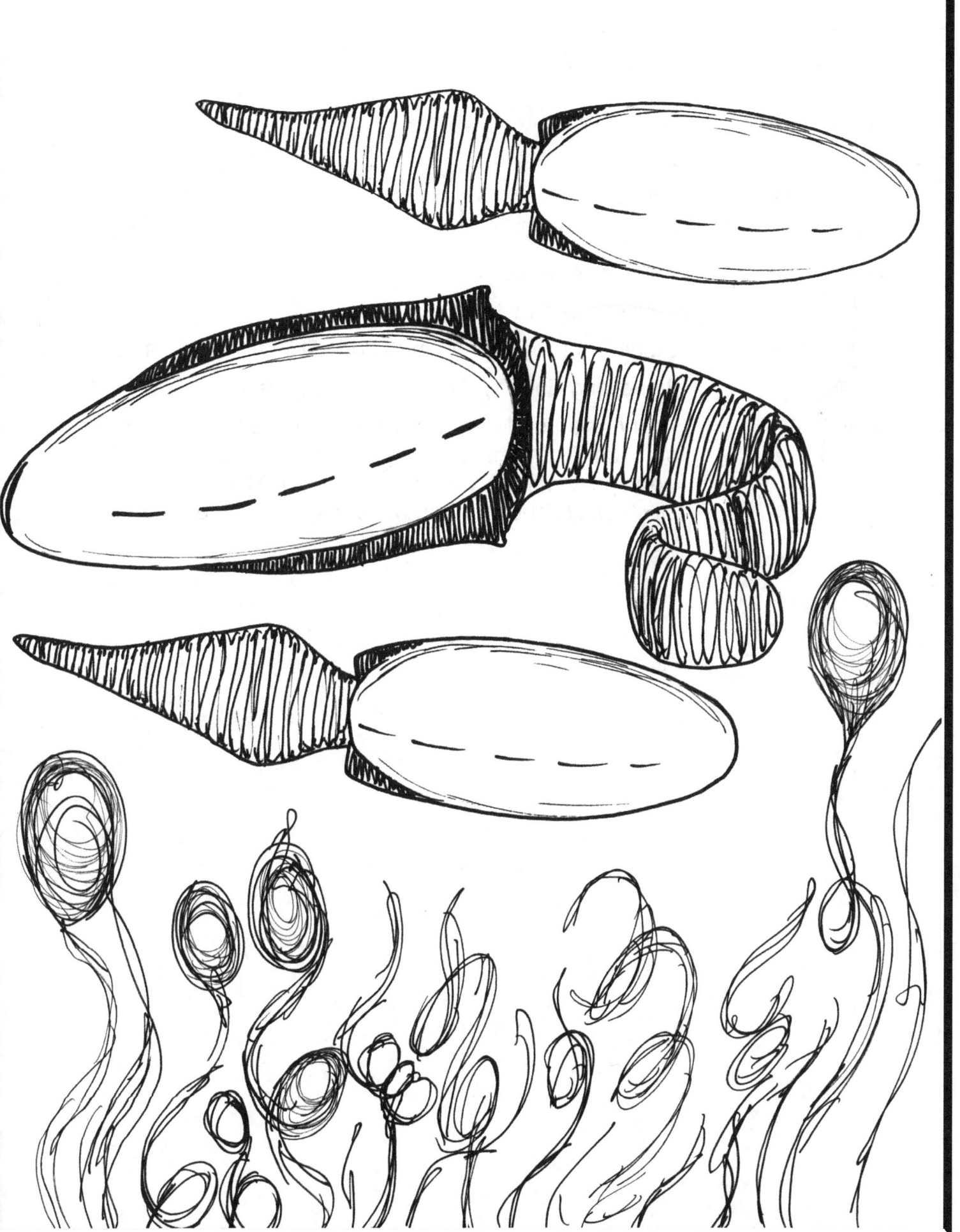

Name   "Form A"

Species   (no formal name given)

Phylum   Chordata

Subphylum   Vetulicolia

Class   Heteromorphida

Family   Heteromorphidae

Size   Around 1 centimeter

Time Period   "Stage 3" of the Cambrian Period, 515 million years ago

Location   Chengjiang County, Yunnan Province, China

Comments   Form A is an undescribed species of differentworm originally found among numerous specimens of Beautiworms. Form A vaguely resembles vetulicolids, save that it has a wrinkled tail characteristic of differentworms, and a large mouth.

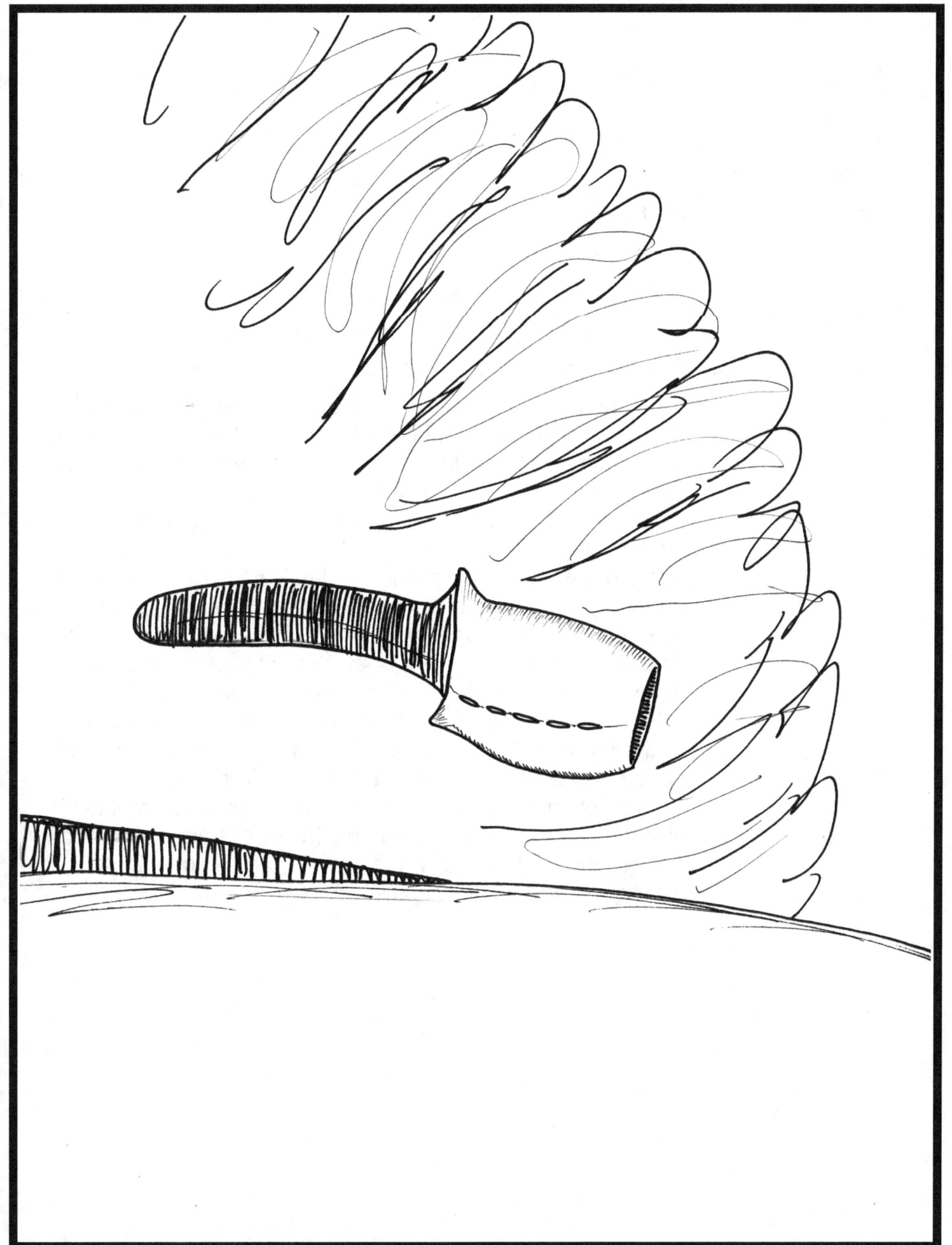

Name	Banffiworm
Species	*Banffia constricta*
Phylum	Chordata
Class	Banffozoa
Family	Banffidae
Size	Up to 10 centimeters in length
Time Period	Middle Cambrian, 508 million years ago.
Location	Burgess Shale, British Columbia
Comments	Even though the Banffiworm, *Banffia constricta*, is one of the lesser known members of the world-famous Burgess Shale Fauna, it is the best known Banffozoan vetulicolian. Of course, given the obscurity of vetulicolians in general, and of Banffozoa in particular, this isn't saying very much, unfortunately.

The banffiworm is a cyndrical animal with a bullet-shaped forebody, and, unique for a tailed animal, has a tail with a kink where the posterior half of the tail was twisted clockwise. Veins in the tail at this kink cross over each other, a situation that would not arise if the tail was simply shaped odd. Researchers theorize that this rotation midway in the tail would have caused the banffiworm to spin while swimming, similar to a bullet discharged from a gun.

As with other vetulicolians, the banffiworm was probably a planktivore or detritivore. The banffiworm is also thought to be gregarious, as its fossils are found slabs containing large groups of up to 40 individuals.

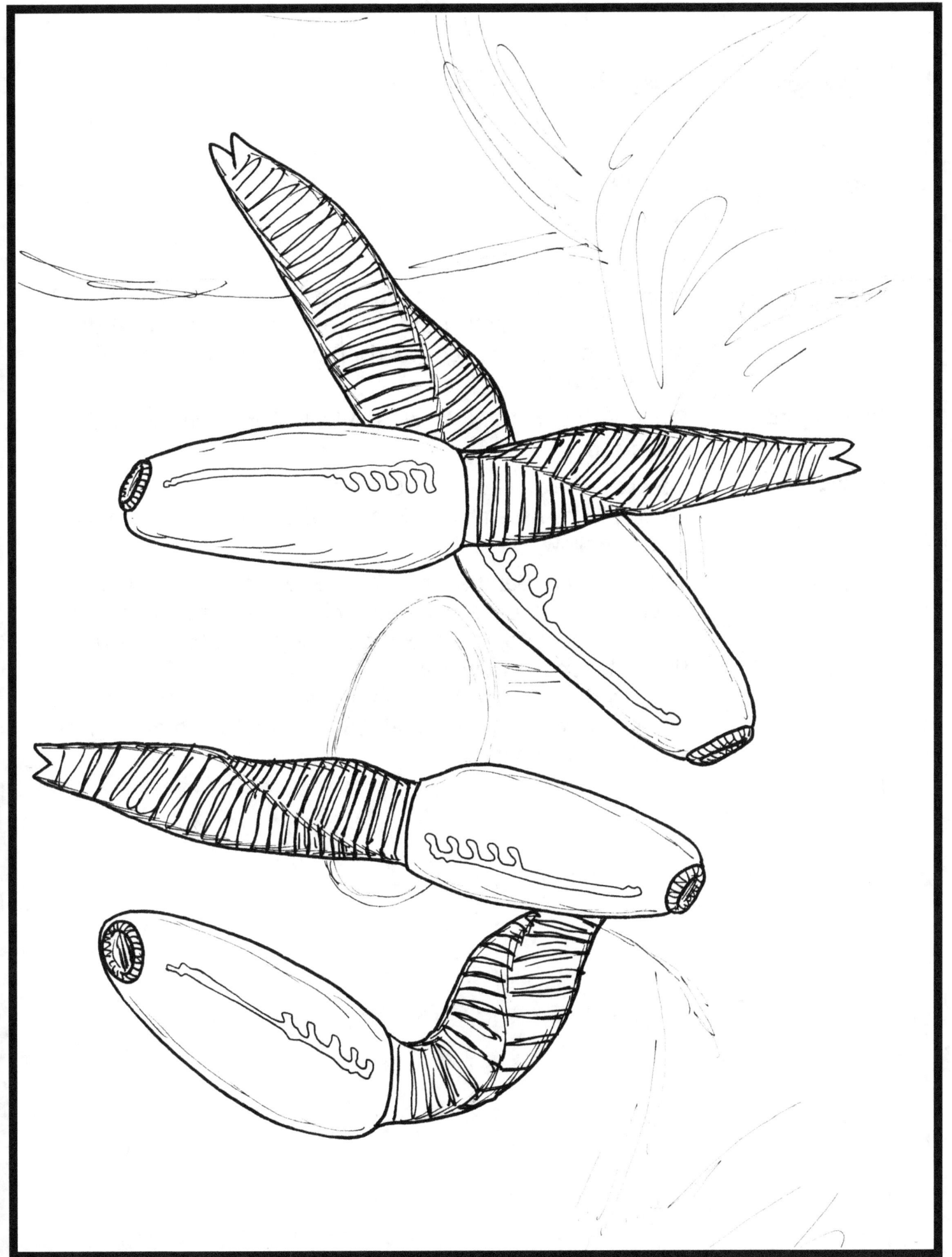

Name	Fattailed Banffiworm
Species	*Banffia episoma*
Phylum	Chordata
Class	Banffozoa
Family	Banffidae
Size	Probably over 10 centimeters: tails range from 4 to 9 centimeters in length (and 2.5 to 4 centimeters in width). Anterior bodies are too poorly preserved to make definite measurements.
Time Period	Stage 5 of Cambrian Series 3, Middle Cambrian, 509 million years ago.
Location	Spence Shale Member, Langston Formation, polymerid Glossopleura Assemblage Zone in the Wellsville Mountains, Miners Hollow, Utah.
Comments	The Fattailed Banffiworm, *Banffia episoma*, is a recently discovered and described vetulicolian from Utah, and is the second vetulicolian described from that state (the first being the Clubworm, *Skeemella*).
	The main difference between the fattailed banffiworm and the banffiworm is the enormous tail of the former which dwarfs its own body.

Name	Clubworm
Species	*Skeemella clavula*
Phylum	Chordata
Class	Vetulicolia
Class	Banffozoa
Family	*incertae sedis*
Size	Estimated to be over 14 centimeters long
Time Period	Middle Cambrian, about 507 million years ago
Location	Drum Mountains, Utah, at a location 30 kilometers northeast of the Wheeler Amphitheatre.
Comments	The anterior portion of the only known fossil of the Clubworm, *Skeemella clavula*, was collected by amateur rockhounds Holly and Ken Skeem, whom researchers honored after the counterslab of the fossil was retrieved.

In life, the clubworm would have been weird-looking even by vetulicolian standards: a small, knot-shaped body dominated by a proportionally ridiculously long tail tipped with a peculiar, twin-pointed structure reminiscent of the telsons of primitive crustaceans and chelicerates.

When the clubworm was described, it was thought to be a vetulicolian in Vetulicolida, possibly related to *Vetulicola*. Later, Richard Aldridge and his cohorts placed the clubworm in Banffozoa as a probable relative of the Banffiworm.

In an inverted irony similar to how the ancientworms were originally described as bivalved arthropods, several researchers doubt the Clubworm's status as a vetulicolian, and instead, suspect it may be a (tail of a) bivalved arthropod. However, this skepticism is tempered by a need to confirm it with a more thorough examination of the holotype and counterslab.

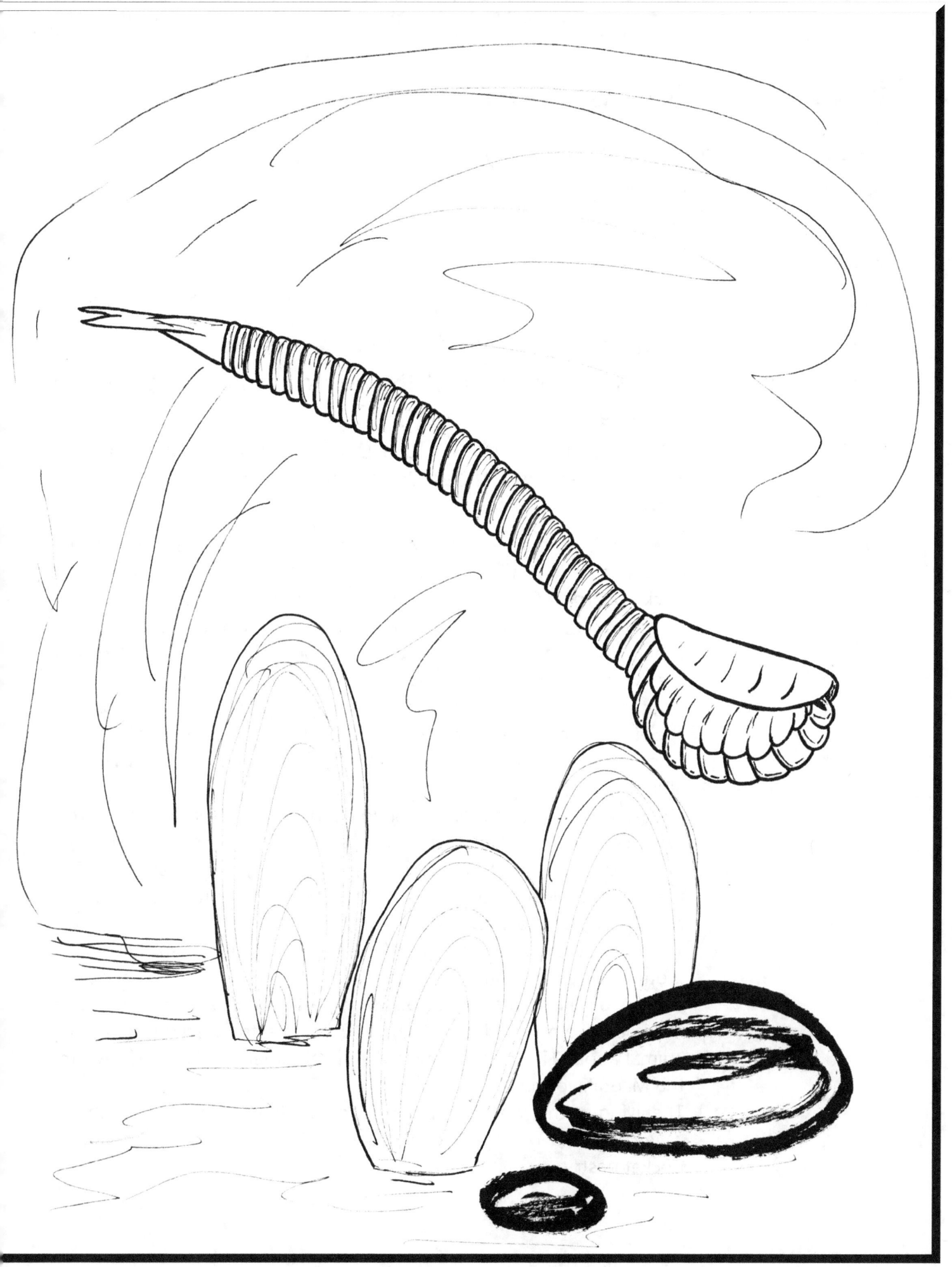

Name	Islandswimmer
Species	*Nesonektris aldridgei*
Phylum	Chordata
Subphylum	Vetulicolia
Class	Vetulicolida
Family	*incertae sedis*
Size	Estimated to be up to 17 centimeters in length
Time Period	Late Botomian Epoch of the Middle Cambrian, 517 million years ago
Location	*Pararaia* janeae zone in the Buck Quarry of the Emu Bay Shale Lagerstätte, near Big Gully, Kangaroo Island, South Australia.
Comments	The Islandswimmer, *Nesonektris aldridgei,* is a recently discovered and described vetulicolid vetulicolian from the *Pararaia* janeae zone in the Buck Quarry of the Emu Bay Shale Lagerstätte, near Big Gully, Kangaroo Island, South Australia. The generic name is a compound Greek word meaning "island swimmer," possibly in reference to how the living animal was obviously well-adapted to swimming in the water column, and how Kangaroo Island being so remote from China. The specific name commemorates the efforts and memory of Richard "Dick" Aldridge for his irreplaceable research in resolving vetulicolian affinities.

The exquisitely preserved, though incomplete fossil specimens allowed researchers to realize that what was originally identified as a coiled gut in the tails of other vetulicolians was actually a notochord. This identification lead researchers to confirm that vetulicolians were a sister-group of Urochordata.

The fossils suggest a very large vetulicolian: the largest specimens are around 15 centimeters in length, after one takes into account the folding of the corpses that according during traumatic burial in a mudslide-like event. This length of 15 cm is extrapolated into a living animal about 17 cm long, which dwarfs all other vetulicolians save for the Magnifiworm.

The living animal would probably have, to a human observer, probably called to mind a tadpole or larval tunicate shaped reminiscent of a pocket pastry.

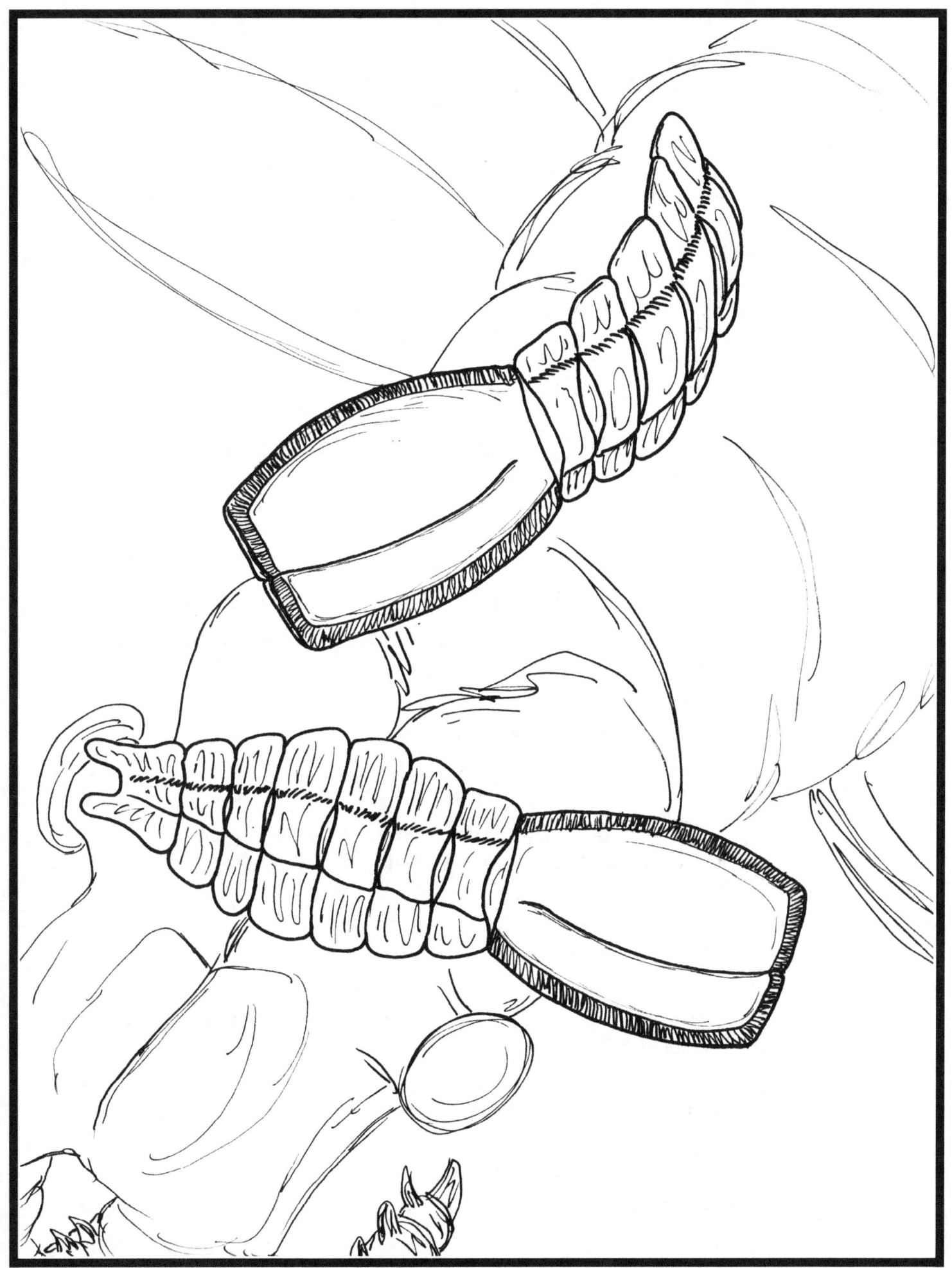

Bibliography

- Ailin, C. H. E. N., et al. "A new vetulicolian from the early Cambrian Chengjiang fauna in Yunnan of China." *Acta Geologica Sinica (English Edition)* 77.3 (2003): 281-287.

- Aldridge, Richard J., et al. "The systematics and phylogenetic relationships of vetulicolians." *Palaeontology* 50.1 (2007): 131-168.

- Briggs, Derek EG, et al. "A new metazoan from the Middle Cambrian of Utah and the nature of the Vetulicolia." *Palaeontology* 48.4 (2005): 681-686.

- Butterfield, N. J. "Vetulicola cuneata from the lower Cambrian Mural Formation, Jasper National Park, Canada." *Palaeontol. Assoc. Newsi* 60 (2005): 17.

- Caron, Jean-Bernard. "Banffia constricta, a putative vetulicolid from the Middle Cambrian Burgess Shale." *Transactions of the Royal Society of Edinburgh: Earth Sciences* 96.02 (2005): 95-111.

- Chen, Feng, Ma, Li, (2003), <u>A New Vetulicolian from the Early Cambrian Chengjiang Fauna in Yunnan of China</u> Acta Geologica Sinica

- García-Bellido, Diego C., et al. "A new vetulicolian from Australia and its bearing on the chordate affinities of an enigmatic Cambrian group." *BMC evolutionary biology* 14.1 (2014): 214.

- Gee, H., 2001. Palaeontology: on being vetulicolian. Nature 414 (6862), 407–409

- Hu, ShiXue, et al. "Biodiversity and taphonomy of the Early Cambrian Guanshan biota, eastern Yunnan." *Science China Earth Sciences* 53.12 (2010): 1765-1773.

- Huilin, Luo, et al. "New vetulicoliids from the Lower Cambrian Guanshan Fauna, Kunming." *Acta Geologica Sinica (English Edition)* 79.1 (2005): 1-6.

- Lacalli, T.C., 2002. Vetulicolians — are they deuterostomes? Chordates? BioEssays 24, 208–211.

- Li, Yu-Jing, et al. "New observations on morphological variation of genus Vetulicola with quadrate carapace from the Cambrian Chengjiang and Guanshan biotas, South China." *Palaeoworla* 24.1 (2015): 36-45.

- Luo, H.L., Fu, X.P., Hu, S.X., Li, Y., Chen, L.Z., You, T., Liu, Q., 2005. New vetulicoliids from the Lower Cambrian Guanshan Fauna, Kunming. Acta Geologica Sinica (English Edition) 79 (1), 1–6.

- Morris, Simon Conway, et al. "Rare primitive deuterostomes from the Cambrian (Series 3) of Utah." *Journal of Paleontology* 89.4 (2015): 631-636.

- Ou, Qiang, et al. "Evidence for gill slits and a pharynx in Cambrian vetulicolians: implications for the early evolution of deuterostomes." *BMC biology* 10.1 (2012): 81.

- Shu, D-G., et al. "Primitive deuterostomes from the Chengjiang Lagerstätte (Lower Cambrian, China)." *Nature* 414.6862 (2001): 419-424.

- Shu, Degan. "On the phylum Vetulicolia." *Chinese Science Bulletin* 50.20 (2005): 2342-

2354.

- Shu, D-G., et al. "The earliest history of the deuterostomes: the importance of the Chengjiang Fossil-Lagerstätte." *Proceedings of the Royal Society of London B: Biological Sciences* 277.1679 (2010): 165-174.
- Vinther, Jakob, M. SMITH, and David AT Harper. "Vetulicolians from the Lower Cambrian Sirius Passet Lagerstätte, North Greenland, and the polarity of morphological characters in basal deuterostomes." *Palaeontology* 54.3 (2011): 711-719.
- Xian-guang, Hou. "Early Cambrian large bivalved arthropods from Chengjiang, eastern Yunnan." *Acta Palaeontologica Sinica* 26.3 (1987): 286-298.
- Yang,J., Hou, X.G., Cong, P.Y., Dong, W., Zhang, Y.X., Luo, M.B., 2010. A new Vetulicoliid from Lower Cambrian, Kunming Yunnan. Acta Palaeontologica Sinica 49 (1), 54–63 (in Chinese, with English abstract).

About the Artist

Stanton F. Fink is a student of Biology and Chinese Medicine, and makes a hobby of drawing monsters and researching flowers, arcane-looking creatures, prehistoric animals, fish, reptiles, birds and the occasional, really grotesque fungal fruiting body.

Stanton grew up and went to school in California and is currently living, drawing, and gardening in Oregon.

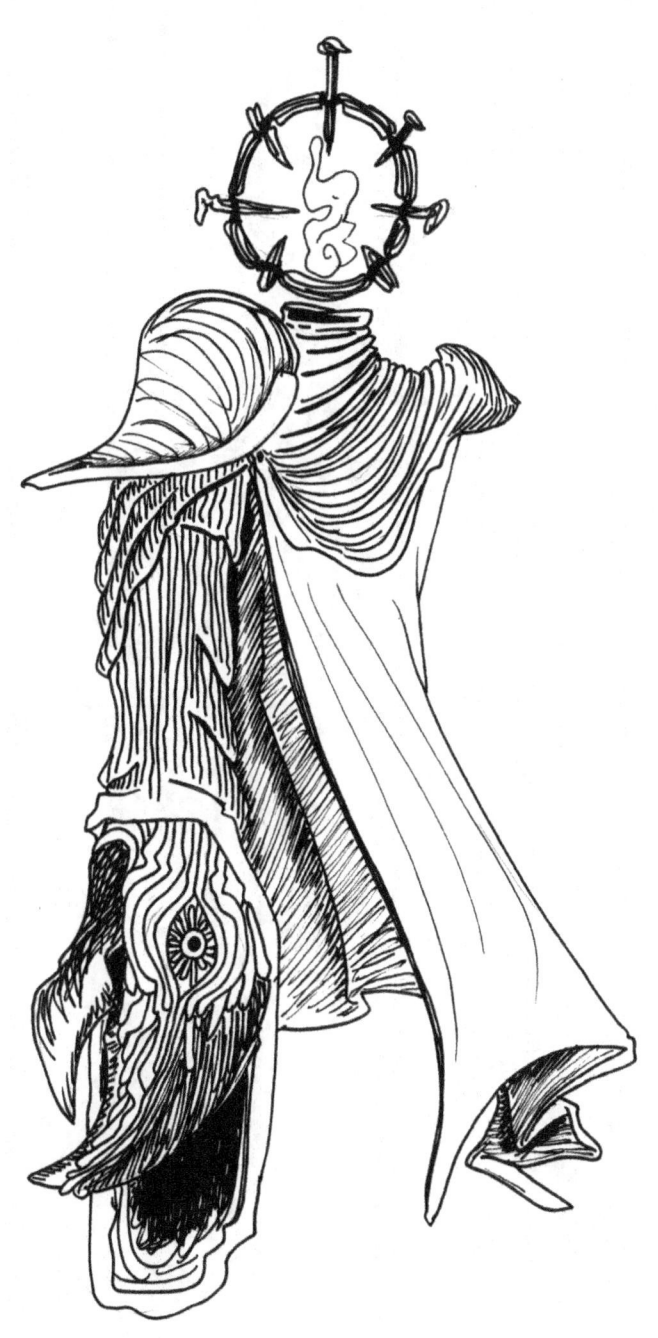

9 781543 299922